EXPERIMENTS with MAGNETISM

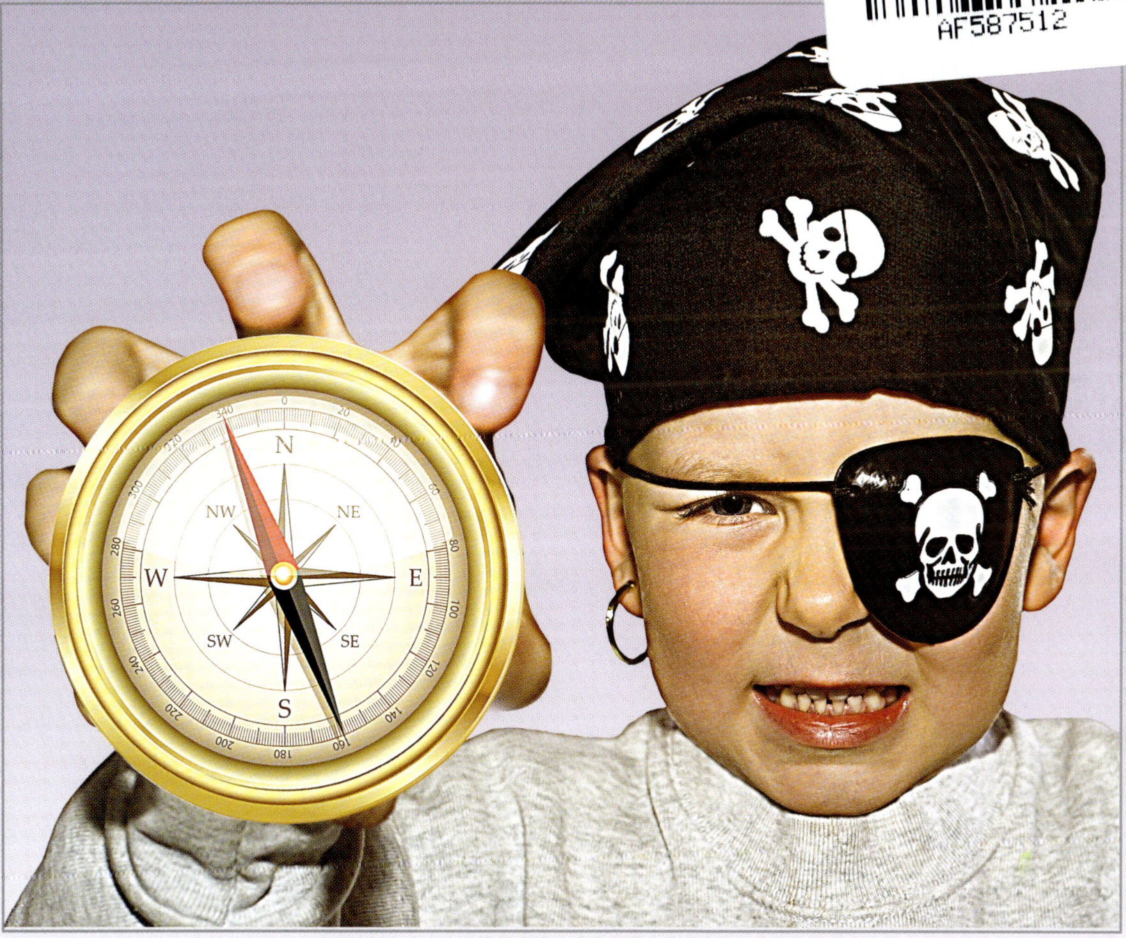

LEARNERS

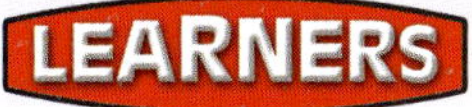

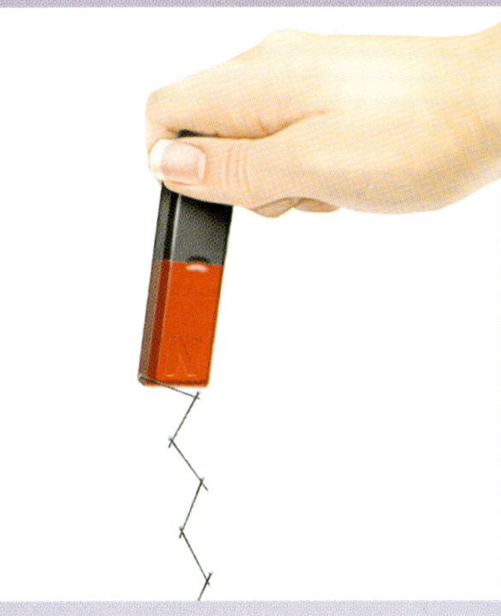

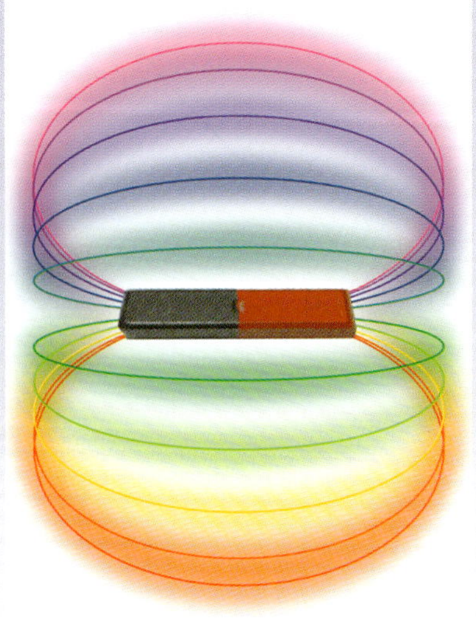

Contents

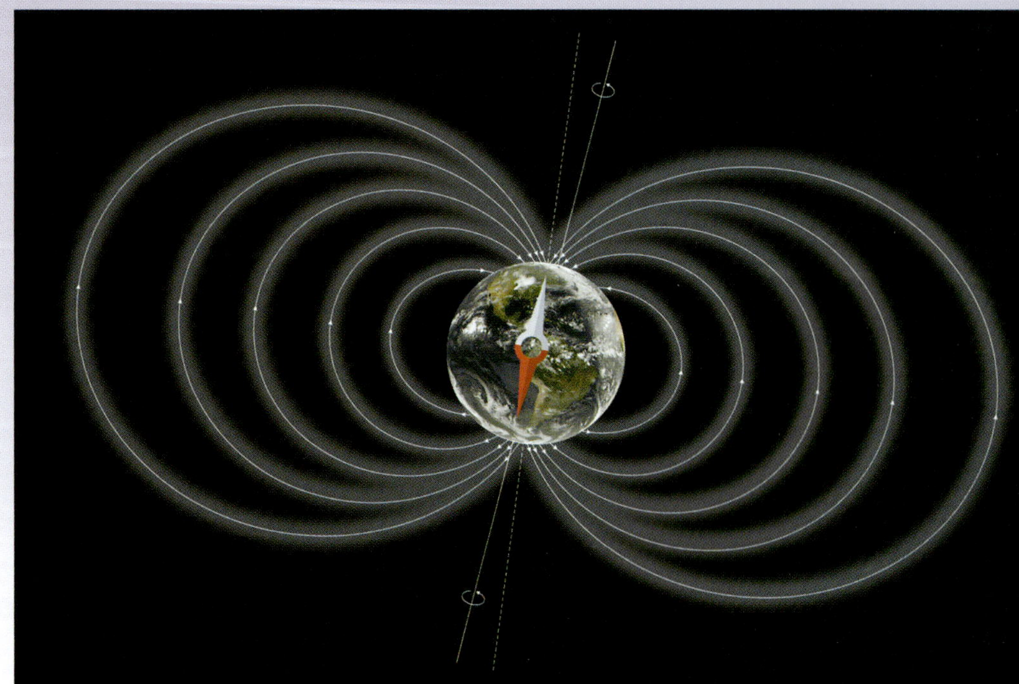

What Are Magnets?

Magnesia is an area near ancient Greece. Here, the Greeks discovered that a kind of black stone attracted pieces of iron. Can you imagine what the Greeks must have felt when they found this happening? Later scientists came to know that this stone is an ore of iron and is called magnetite. Anything that had this property of attracting iron came to be known as a magnet.

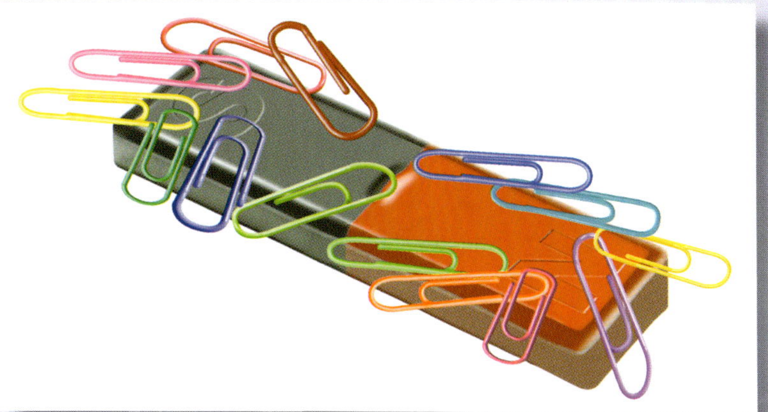

The magnets you commonly come across are in the shape of *bar magnets* or *horseshoe magnets*. Magnets are generally made of iron or steel. They can also be made of nickel or cobalt. A specific combination of aluminium, nickel, iron, cobalt and copper, called *Alnico* makes very strong magnets.

Have you seen a magnet? Doors of refrigerators have magnet linings. The magnet helps to keep the door tightly shut. With your mother's permission open the refrigerator door and check this out. Open the door slightly and let go. The door should close by itself. Magnets are good playthings. But let us not play with the refrigerator magnet. Go to a shop that sells scientific instruments and get yourself a bar magnet.

Magnets and magnetic substances

You will need:

- a magnet
- some paper clips
- a pen or a pencil
- a piece of paper

1. Hold the magnet near the clips. What happens?
2. Shake the magnet, first slowly, and then vigorously. Do the clips fall down?
3. Hold the magnet to the pen or the pencil. What do you find? Touch the papers with the magnet. What happens?
4. Touch the things around you with the magnet and note what you see.
5. Pretend you are an ancient Greek and write down an explanation for what you observed just now.
6. Read further to see whether what you thought is what scientists think. (The Greeks thought that there are tiny hooks in a magnet to catch pieces of iron!)

A magnet has an invisible force with which it *pulls* or *pushes* certain things. This property of magnets to pull or push things is called *magnetism.*

All things however do not respond to magnetic force. The things that do respond are called *magnetic substances*. The things that do not respond to magnets are called *nonmagnetic substances*. Let us find out the kind of things magnets attract.

You will need:

- paper clip, nail, glass, key, coin, tin, paper, cloth, pencil, knife
- a bar magnet

1. Touch the magnet to each of the items.
2. Record your results in the table below.
3. Notice what happens when you touch a magnet with another magnet.

Object under test		Magnetic substance	
Name	Made of	Yes	No
paper clip	iron		

Know Your Magnet

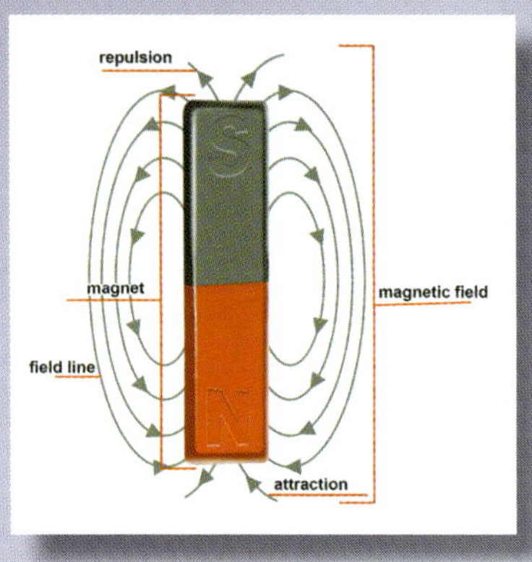

Magnetism cannot be directly sensed by us. It cannot be seen, touched, heard or smelt. The only way to learn more about magnets is to note what a magnet does in various situations. Let us do this step by step.

Magnets can separate magnetic and nonmagnetic things. Let us check.

You will need:

- wood shavings
- paper clips
- a bar magnet
- a glass of water

1. Mix the paper clips with the wood shavings.
2. Move the magnet over the mixture. What happens?
3. Put the clips in the glass of water. Dip the magnet in the water. What happens?
4. Put back the clips in the water. Move the magnet around the outer surface of the glass. What do you find?

Many food and chemical industries use magnetic separators to make sure that iron particles are not accidentally mixed into their products. Thanks to the magnetic separators that we get safer food.

The force of attraction of a magnet is not uniform along its length. Check it out.

You will need:

- a bar magnet
- some paper clips

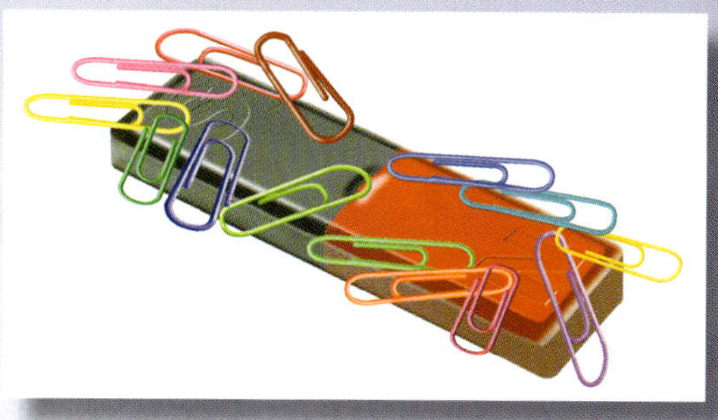

1. Place the magnet on a table. Sprinkle the paper clips on it. What happens?
2. Take the magnet, turn it upside down and shake gently. What do you find? Where do the maximum number of clips stick?

The ends of the magnet to which most of the clips remain stuck are the centres of attraction of the magnet. They are called the *poles of the magnet.* The middle of a magnet has zero attraction.

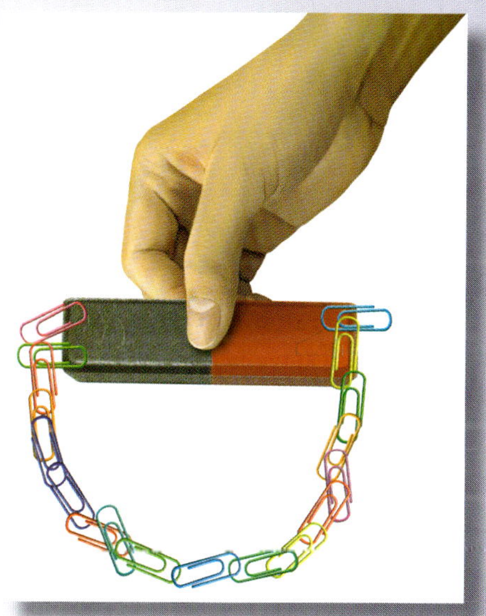

All magnets have two poles. Let us name the poles.

You will need:

- a bar magnet
- thread

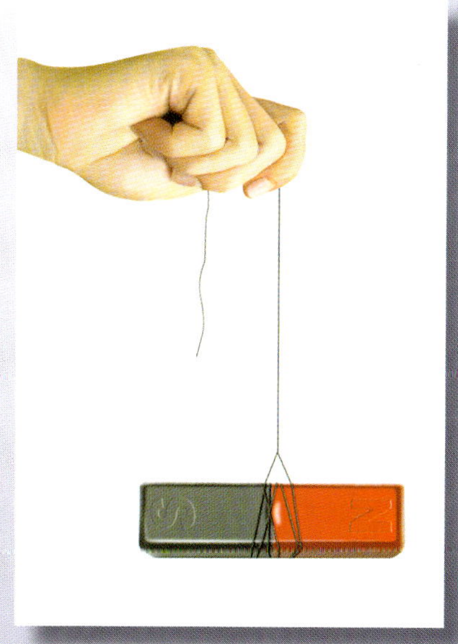

1. Wind the thread to the middle of the magnet and tie a knot. Suspend it from your fingers so that it hangs freely. The magnet should be horizontal.
2. When the magnet is steady, note the direction in which its axis points. Is one end pointing towards the north?

This is the north-seeking pole or the *north pole*. The other pole is the south-seeking pole or the *south pole*. They are often marked as *N* and *S*.

Do magnets always attract? Check it out.

You will need:

- 2 bar magnets (A and B)

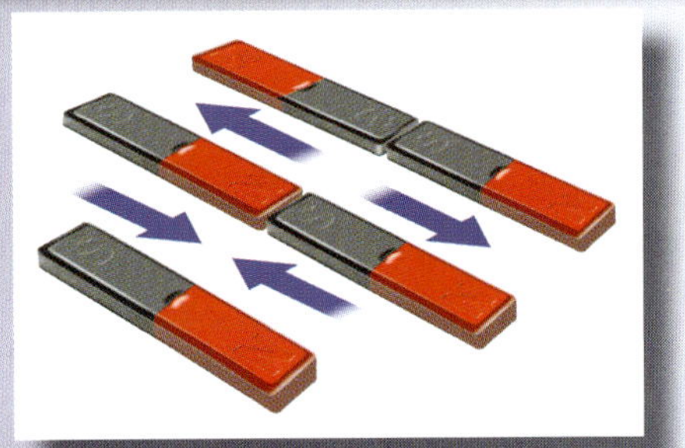

1. Keep magnet A on the table. Bring one end of magnet B close to one end of magnet A. How does A react?
2. Take the other end of B to the same end of A. What does A do now?
3. Repeat steps 1 and 2 at the other end of magnet A. What do you notice?

Your observation can be explained by saying, *opposite poles of a magnet attract*, i.e., north pulls south and *similar poles repel*, i.e., north pushes away north.

Try this

If you have two similar looking bars, one a magnet and another a piece of iron, can you find out which one is the magnet without using anything else? If you know the poles of one magnet, can you find out the poles of all other magnets?

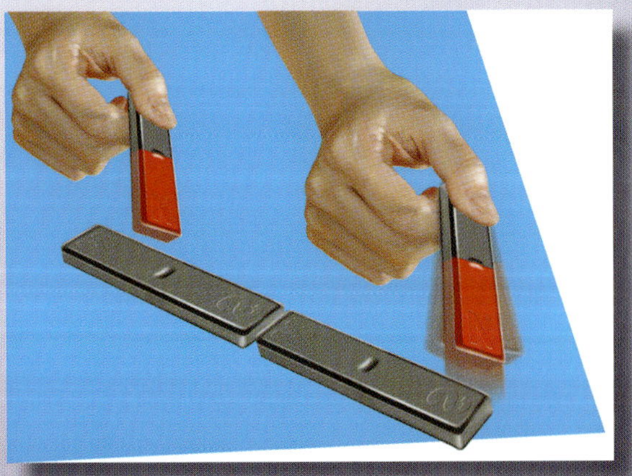

Magnets can make magnets. Let us check.

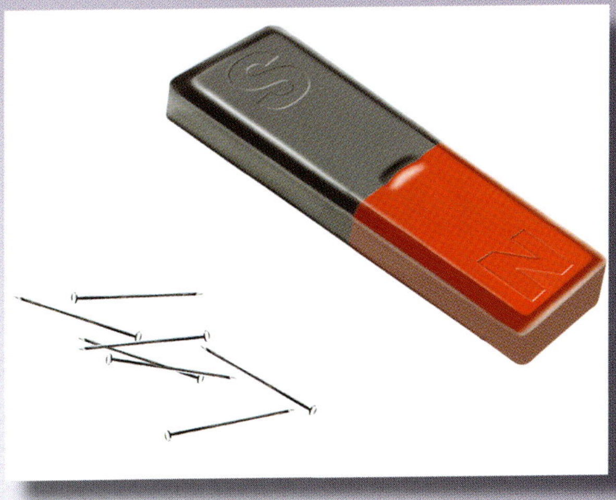

You will need:

- pins
- a bar magnet

1. Bring the head of a pin close to the magnet. The pin should stick to it.
2. Bring the head of a second pin close to the tail of the first pin. Does it stick?
3. Now bring the head of a third pin to the tail of the second, so as to form a chain.
4. Carefully pull the first pin off the magnet. What happens? Do the pins stay together? Have the pins turned into small magnets?
5. Break the chain and carefully put the pins on the table. Bring the head of one pin to that of the second. What happens? Take it to the tail of the second. What happens now? Try with the third pin.
6. Make the chain again and separate it from the magnet. How long do the pins remain in the chain?

You must have seen that the pin magnets you just made, lost their magnetism after some time. These are *temporary magnets*. How long a temporary magnet can hold its magnetism depends on the material of the magnetic substance. *Steel* can retain its magnetism for longer periods of time than *iron*.

Make your own magnet

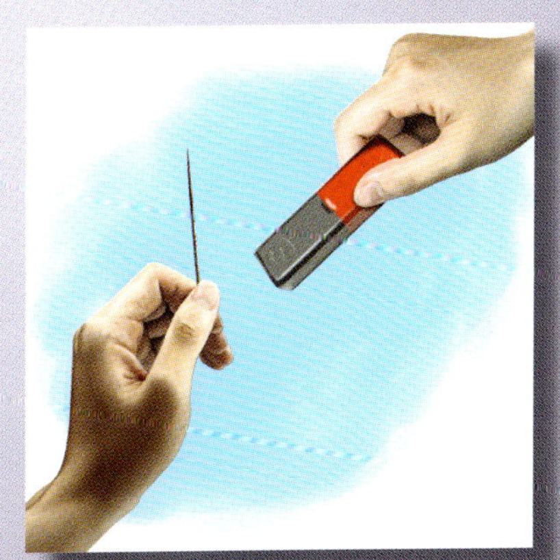

You will need:

- a steel needle
- a bar magnet
- paper clips

1. Hold the steel needle near the paper clips. Do they stick to the needle? Be sure that the needle is not magnetised as yet.
2. Hold the needle in one hand and the magnet in another. Stroke the needle with the north pole of the magnet, starting from the middle and moving to the eye of the needle.
3. Repeat this 20-30 times. Always stroke in one direction. Do not drag the magnet back and forth.
4. Use the south pole of the magnet and stroke the other end of the needle in the same way.
5. Touch the paper clips with the needle. What happens?
6. Bring the eye of the needle near the south pole of the bar magnet. What do you notice? Repeat this with the north pole. Do you know the poles of your magnetised needle? Mark them.

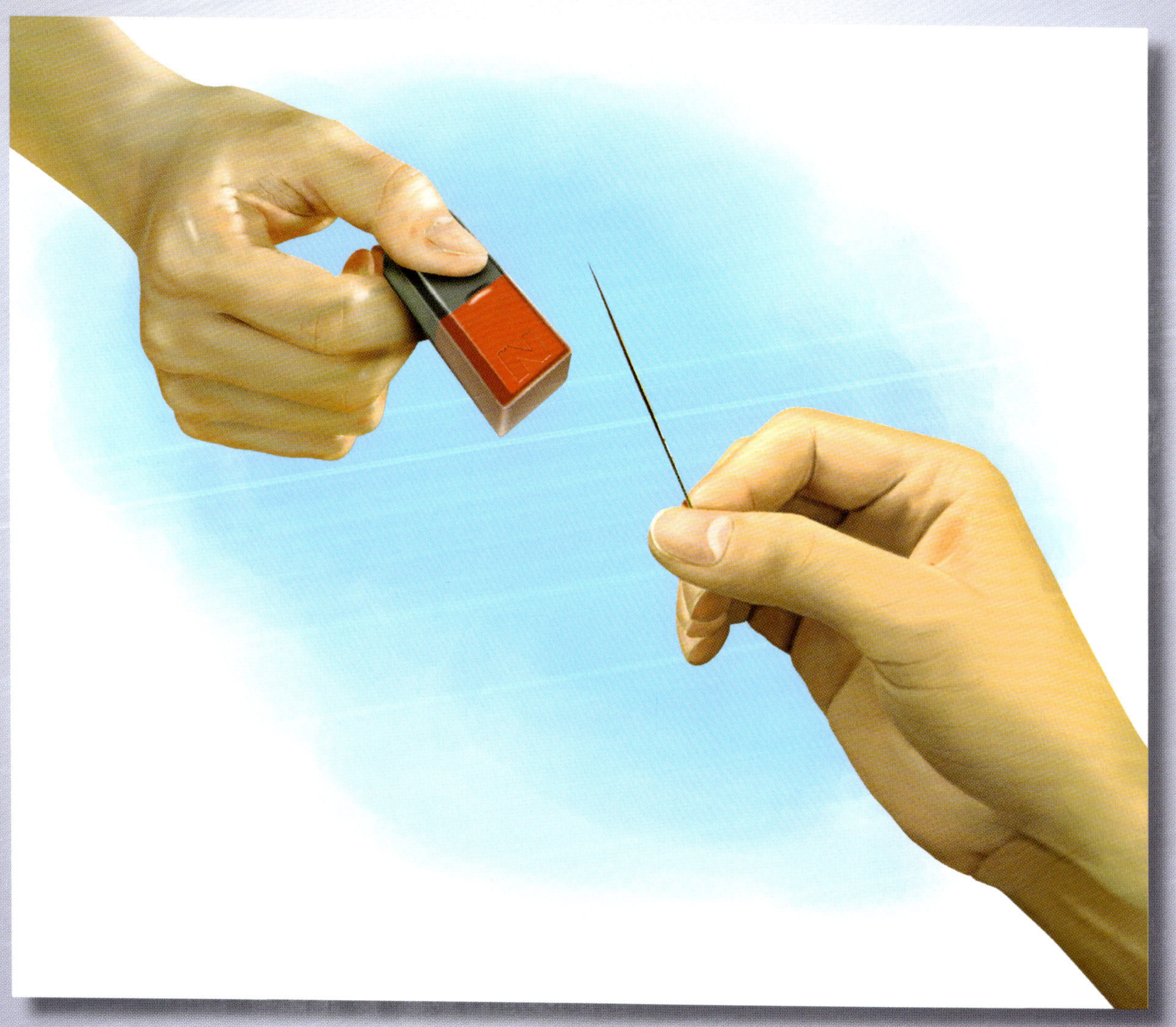

Magnetic Fun

Now that you know your magnet, let us have some magnetic fun.

Hit the bull's eye: a game to test your aim.

You will need:

- friends
- a piece of cardboard
- a bar magnet
- 5 nails
- sellotape

1. Tape the magnet firmly on the cardboard and hang it from a wall at the eye level.
2. Stand two feet away from the wall and take turns to throw the nails so that they stick to the magnet.
3. The one who does it in the least number of attempts, wins.

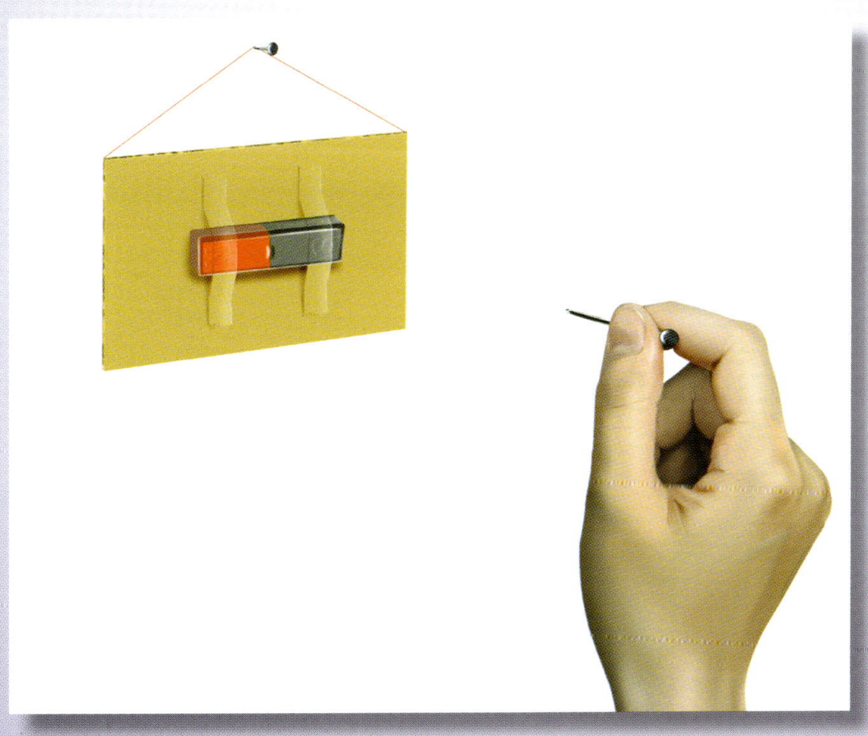

A floating doll: An anti-gravity equipment.

You will need:

- a bar magnet
- a paper clip
- coloured paper
- a pair of scissors
- thread
- sellotape

1. Make a tiny paper doll and fix it to the clip.
2. Tie one end of a 5-inch piece of thread to the doll. Tape the other end of the thread to the table.
3. Slowly bring the magnet close to the doll and raise it. You are not allowed to touch it. Make the doll stand up. How long can you make her float?

Fishing for roles

You will need:

- friends
- sheets of coloured paper
- paper clips
- a pair of scissors
- a cardboard box
- a pen or a pencil
- thread
- a magnet
- a stick

1. Make 20 fishes from the sheets of coloured paper.
2. Attach a paper clip to each fish.

3. On the back of each fish, write things that can be acted out – jump like a kangaroo, pretend you are walking on the moon, or driving on a crowded road, suppose you are a magnet, and other challenging things that you would like to act out.
4. Put all the fishes in the cardboard box.
5. Tie the thread to the magnet. Attach the other end of the thread to the stick. This is your fishing line.
6. Sit in a circle and keep the fish box in the middle. Take turns in fishing out a fish. If you catch more than one fish, take the top one.
7. Read aloud what is written at the back of the fish and act it out.

Draw a face

You will need:

- iron filings
- a magnet
- a piece of paper on which the outline of a man's face is drawn.
- a small bottle with its lid.

1. You can get iron filings from shops where iron grills are made and welding is done. Get some in the bottle.
2. Put a few pinches of iron filings on the outline drawn on the paper. Lift the page carefully and slide your magnet under the picture.
3. Move the magnet to 'draw' with the iron filings, hair, eyebrows, beard and moustache.

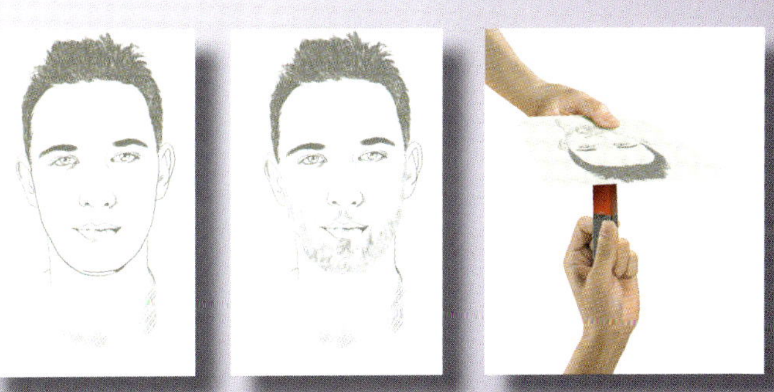

Remember to put the iron filings back into the bottle. You will need it for other experiments.

Around a Magnet

You must have noticed by now that as soon as you bring a magnet near a paper clip, the clip jumps and sticks to the magnet. The north pole of a magnet automatically moves away when the north pole of another magnet comes near it. Obviously, magnets have some power that can pass through space and affect other magnets and magnetic materials near it. This region around which a magnet has its influence is called the magnetic field.

Is this influence uniform along the magnetic field? How far does it spread? To find an answer, let us repeat an experiment we have already done.

You will need:

- a bar magnet
- pins

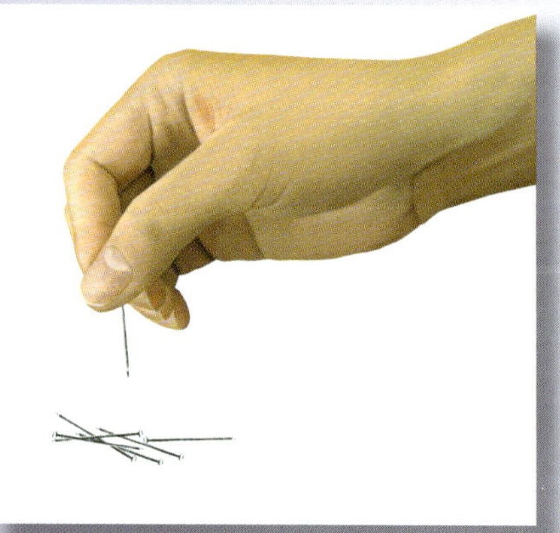

1. Pick a pin with the magnet.
2. Add another pin to the tail of the first pin. It sticks.
3. Keep forming the chain.

How many pins can the magnet hold? After a point, the attraction becomes too small even to hold the weight of a pin.

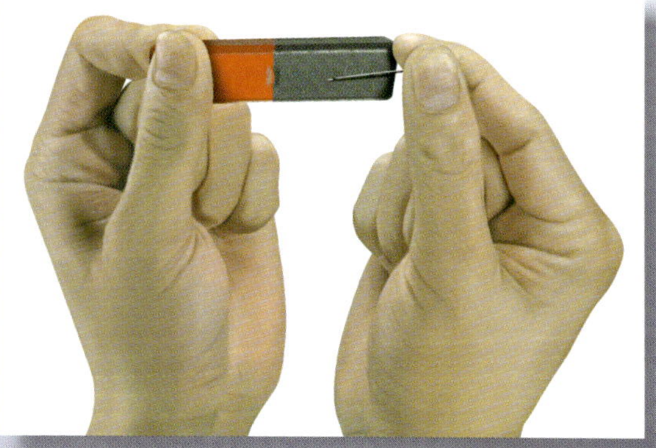

We find that magnetic attraction decreases as we go further away from a magnet. To have a proper idea of how magnetic force is distributed, let us experiment.

You will need:

- a bar magnet
- iron filings
- paper
- a brush

1. Put the magnet on a table and cover it with a piece of paper.
2. Slowly sprinkle the iron filings on the paper. Tap the paper gently. What do you find? The iron filings should form a pattern around the magnet. The lines formed by the filings are called the *lines of force* of a magnet. By looking at the distribution of the iron filings, what can you say about the magnetic force?
3. Try to move the iron filings with the brush. Do you find that the filings closest to the ends of the magnet are the hardest to move? If you have read chapter 2, I am sure you know your magnet well enough to know why this happens.

Is the pattern made by the iron filings going to change when there are two magnets? Check.

You will need:

- 2 bar magnets
- iron filings
- a piece of paper

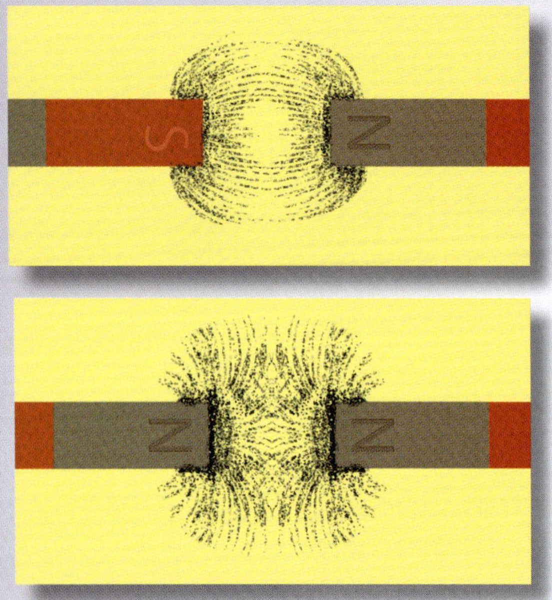

1. Place the two magnets on the table so that the north pole of one faces the south pole of the other. Cover them with the paper. Carefully sprinkle the iron filings on the paper and tap gently. What do you find?
2. Slowly try to pull the magnets apart. What happens to the lines of force?
3. Remove the paper from the magnets. Turn one magnet around so that the like poles of both the magnets face each other. Put them about an inch apart and cover them with the paper. Sprinkle the iron filings on the paper. Note the pattern. Is there any magnetic force in the region between the two like poles?

How will the field pattern look when the north pole of one magnet is joined to the south pole of the other?

What happens to the magnetic field when a metal object is brought near a magnet? Check.

You will need:

- 2 bar magnets
- 2 sheets of paper
- iron filings
- an iron or steel button
- a plastic button

1. Put the magnets on the two sides of a table. Cover them with the sheets of paper and sprinkle both the sheets of paper with the iron filings.

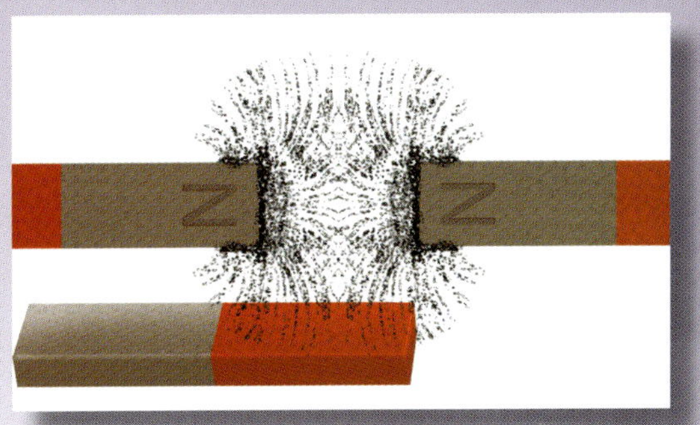

2. Gently push the metal button under one of the sheets of paper so as to touch one end of the magnet. Push the plastic button next to the other magnet.
3. Tap the iron filings. Is there any change in the field pattern in the two cases?

A magnet's field of force can be changed if magnetic things are brought near the magnet. What happens is that the iron button, being magnetic, attracts the magnetic lines of force around it, while the plastic button is nonmagnetic, and is therefore simply ignored by the magnet.

Can a magnetic field be blocked? Let us find out.

You will need:

- a magnet
- some paper clips
- a piece of cardboard
- a metal lid

1. Hold one end of the magnet near the clips. How many clips does it pick up?
2. Put the cardboard next to the end of the magnet and repeat step 1. How many clips does the magnet pick up this time?
3. Hold the metal lid next to the magnet. Bring the magnet near the clips. How many clips are picked up?

From what we saw, it can be said that the lines of force passed through the cardboard, but could not cross the metal lid and influence the paper clips. The lid *blocked* or *shielded* the magnetic force. Materials like iron and steel can be used to shield things from the influence of magnets. They are called *magnetic shields*.

The Inside Story

So far we have studied the influence of a magnet in a region around it. But what is inside a magnet? Let us break a magnet into two and find out.

You will need:

- a magnet
- a metal hairpin
- a paper clip
- pliers

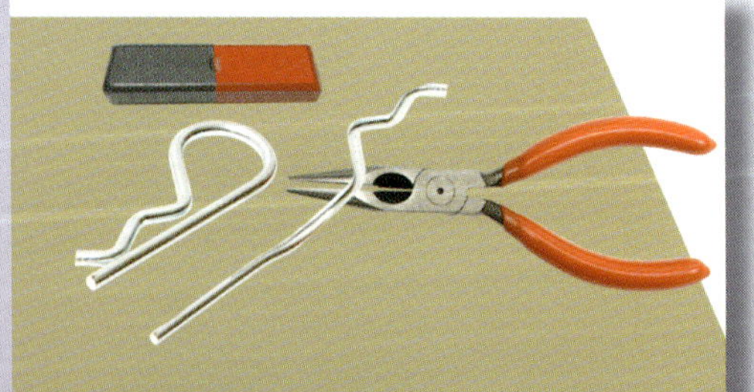

1. Straighten the hairpin with the pliers. Do not bother about the ripples. Magnetise the pin by stroking it with your magnet. (For directions see 'Make your own magnet' on page 10)
2. Bring the hairpin near the paper clip. Is it behaving like a magnet?
3. Very slowly bend the centre of the hairpin back and forth with the pliers until it breaks into two.
4. Find out if the two pieces of hairpins are magnets or not.

If you keep on breaking a magnet into two, each time you will get smaller and smaller magnets. If you keep on breaking a magnet, guess what you will ultimately be left with? You will have a single atom which will behave as a tiny magnet. So you can say that a larger magnet is actually made of numerous tiny magnets.

Now, let us break a plain, nonmagnetised hairpin into two.

You will need:

- a magnet
- a metal hairpin
- a paper clip
- pliers

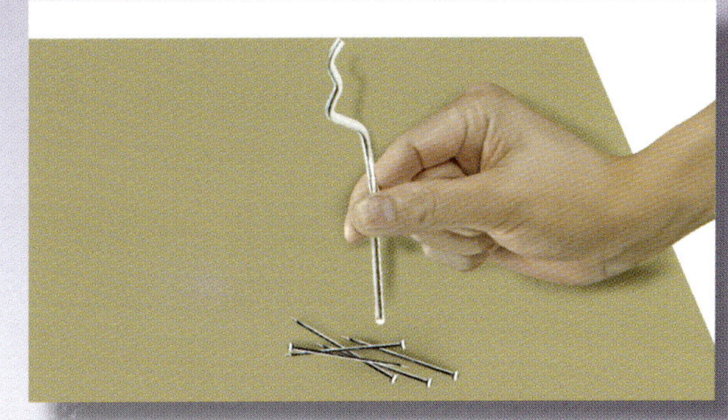

1. Test the hairpin to find out if it is a magnet.
2. Bring it close to the magnet to make sure that it is magnetic.
3. Straighten it, and as before break it at the centre with the help of the pliers.
4. Test the two broken parts. Are the two pieces magnetic? Are they magnets?

I am sure, even before doing the experiment you knew that the two pieces of the broken hairpin were not magnets. Do not get bored. Remember that a good scientist checks everything.

Suppose you keep breaking into two, a nonmagnetised iron piece, it is obvious that you will get smaller and smaller nonmagnetised iron bits. But finally when you end up with an atom, what do you find? It is strange, but you will be left with an iron atom which really behaves like a magnet!

Is it then true that things like iron are also made of a very large number of tiny magnets? Is there any difference between the tiny magnets in a larger magnet and those in a nonmagnetised piece of iron, which can explain why the two behave differently when brought near a paper clip? What can it be?

In a magnet, the tiny magnets inside are all organised with their **N** pointing in one direction and their **S** in the opposite direction. This gives rise to a pull. In a plain, nonmagnetised iron the tiny magnets are disorganised. The effect of this is that there is no resultant pull and so no magnetic field.

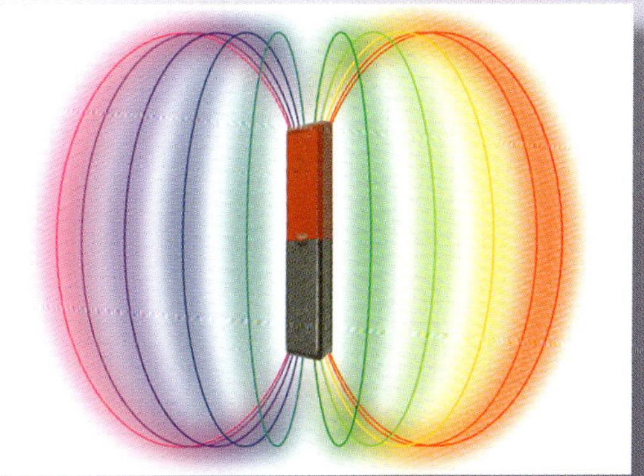

Try this

What were you actually doing when you were stroking a plain iron nail to magnetise it? Why was it necessary to stroke in one direction? Why does a paper clip stick to a magnet?

Can the magnetism of a magnet be destroyed? Yes, if you can disorganise the tiny magnets inside the magnet. Let us experiment.

You will need:

- a magnet
- a nail
- a paper clip
- a candle
- a matchbox
- a pair of tongs

1. Magnetise the nail. Bring it close to the paper clip and check whether it is magnetised.
2. Throw the magnetised nail hard on to the floor. Check whether it is still a magnet. Repeat this several times. Does the nail still attract the clip?
3. Magnetise the nail again.
4. Light the candle. Hold the nail with a pair of tongs and heat it over the flame.

Be careful while heating. Test for its magnetism. What do you find?

When a magnet is hit or heated, the tiny magnets inside it get disorganised. So the magnet loses it magnetic attraction. The magnet is *demagnetised.*

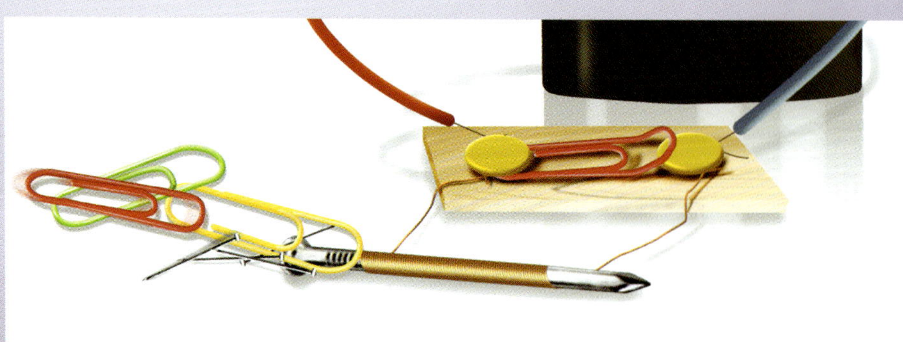

The Earth Is a Magnet

Did you know that the earth is a giant magnet? Let us try to find out.

You will need:

- a bar magnet
- thread

1. Wind one end of the thread several times around the middle of the bar magnet and tie a knot. Hold the other end of the thread between your fingers so that the magnet hangs freely. If suspended like this, it should be balanced and remain parallel to the ground.
2. When the magnet comes to rest, note the direction in which it points. Why does the magnet point in a definite direction?
3. Move around the room with the suspended magnet and check the direction in which it points each time.

4. What happens when you go outside?

You must have noticed that your magnet comes to rest always pointing in the same direction. This happens because your magnet is under the influence of the magnetic field of the earth's magnet.

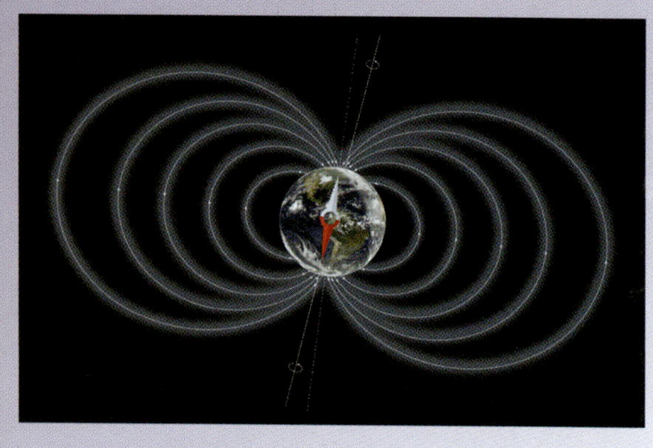

Compasses, which are freely suspended magnetic needles, have been used throughout the ages by navigators for finding directions. A compass needle always points towards the north pole of the earth's magnet. The magnetic poles of the earth are slightly shifted from the geographic north and south poles. You can use your compass to find the angle of difference between the magnetic north and the geographic north. (The North Star will tell you where the north is.) This difference is called ***variation***.

Navigators have to make a correction for this variation of the compass in order to locate their position.

Try this

Does the compass needle always give true directions? What happens inside a steel factory or a place where there is iron ore in the earth? Can you shield your compass from these magnetic fields?

Make your own compass

You will need:

- a magnet
- a needle
- a cork
- a glass of water
- sellotape
- detergent

1. Magnetise the needle. Test it to see if it is magnetised.
2. Tape the needle to the cork.
3. Float the cork in the glass of water. Add a little detergent to help it float freely. In what direction does your compass needle point?
4. Take it to other parts of the room and outside. Does it always point in the north-south direction?

Electromagnets

We know that magnets can be made with other magnets. Can you make a magnet without a magnet? Let us try.

You will need:

- a big nail
- 2 insulated wires, one 15 inches and the other 8 inches long
- a 9-volt battery
- 2 board pins
- a thick piece of cardboard or wooden block
- a paper clip
- sellotape
- pins

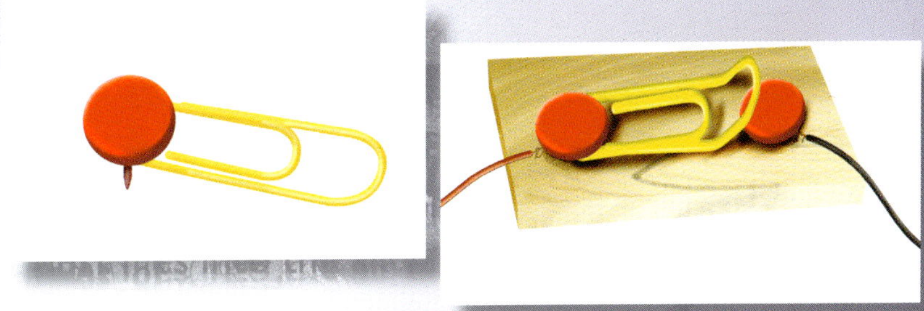

1. Bend the paper clip as shown in the figure. Pin one end of it to the board with a board pin. Put the other board pin about 1½ inches away. This makes a simple switch.
2. Remove one inch of insulation from the ends of the wires. Wind the longer wire around the nail 25 times and tape it in place.
3. Connect one end of the wire to one end of the battery. Put the other end of the wire round one of the board pins.
4. Connect the shorter wire to the other end of the battery. Fasten the free end to the second board pin. Press the pins down firmly.
5. Now press the paper clip switch down on the board pin. This turns the switch ON. Bring some paper pins near the nail. What do you find? (Caution: keep the switch ON only for a few seconds. Otherwise it will drain your battery.)
6. Release the switch. What happens?

What you just made is an electric current magnet or an *electromagnet*. The battery produces an electric current. When this current flows through the wire, the nail becomes magnetised. So an electric current produces magnetism.
To be sure, let us check again.

You will need:

- a compass
- a 9-volt battery
- a piece of insulated wire
- tape

1. Remove an inch of insulation from the ends of the wire. Tape one end of the wire to a terminal of the battery.
2. Put the compass (to make a home-made compass, see directions on page 25) on the table and hold the wire over it.
3. Touch the free end of the wire to the other terminal of the battery. What do you find? Does your compass needle turn?
4. Remove the wire from the battery. Does the needle return to its original position?

As there were no magnets around, the compass must have responded to the magnetic field of the current in the wire.

How strong is an electromagnet?

You will need:

- 2 large nails
- 2 insulated wires
- two 9-volt batteries
- an ON/OFF switch
- sellotape
- pins

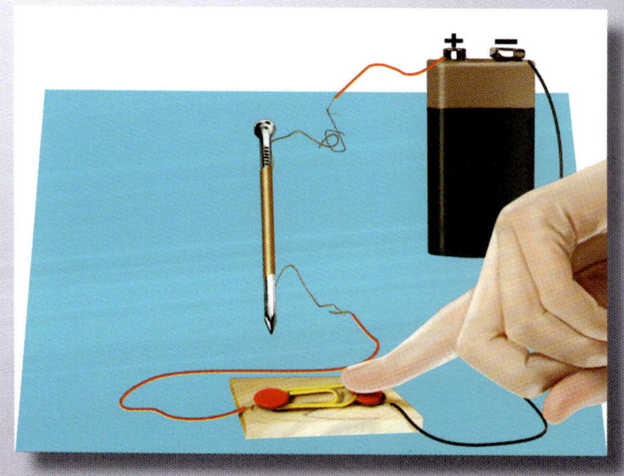

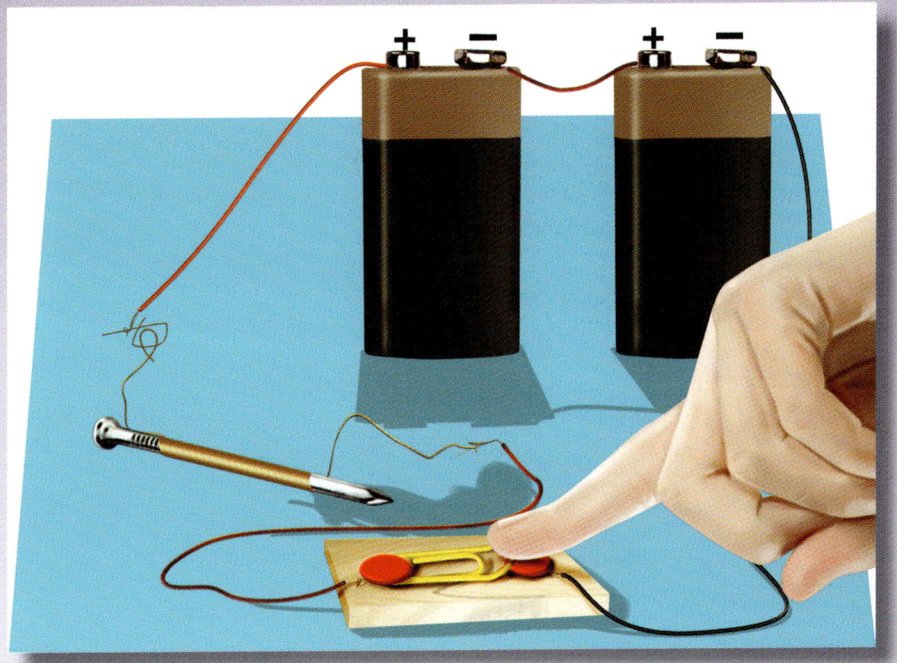

1. Remove an inch of insulation from the ends of the wires. Wrap one nail with 25 turns and another with 50 turns of wire.
2. Connect the switch to the battery and the nail with 25 turns, as shown on page 26.
3. Press the switch clip ON to make an electromagnet. Bring the pins near the electromagnet. How many pins stick to the magnet?
4. Now take off the 25-turn nail and connect the 50-turn nail in its place.
5. Press the switch ON to make another electromagnet. How many pins does this magnet draw?
6. Now connect the 50-turn nail to the two batteries as shown. The positive end of one battery should be connected to the negative end of the other.
7. Put the switch ON. How many pins does the magnet draw this time?

The strength of an electromagnet depends on the strength of the electric current passing through it. Two 9-volt batteries connected as shown, produce twice the current in the wire as one 9-volt battery could do. So the electromagnet made with two batteries is stronger.

The strength of an electromagnet also depends on the number of turns of wire. More turns produce stronger electromagnets.

What happens when the current passing through an electromagnet is turned off?

When you switched off the current, the nail was probably still acting like a magnet. This is because *iron* can hold magnetism for some time. If you had used a piece of *soft iron* instead, you would find that the magnetism disappeared as soon as the current was switched off. Soft iron magnets are *temporary magnets*. It is difficult to show this experimentally as soft iron is difficult to find.

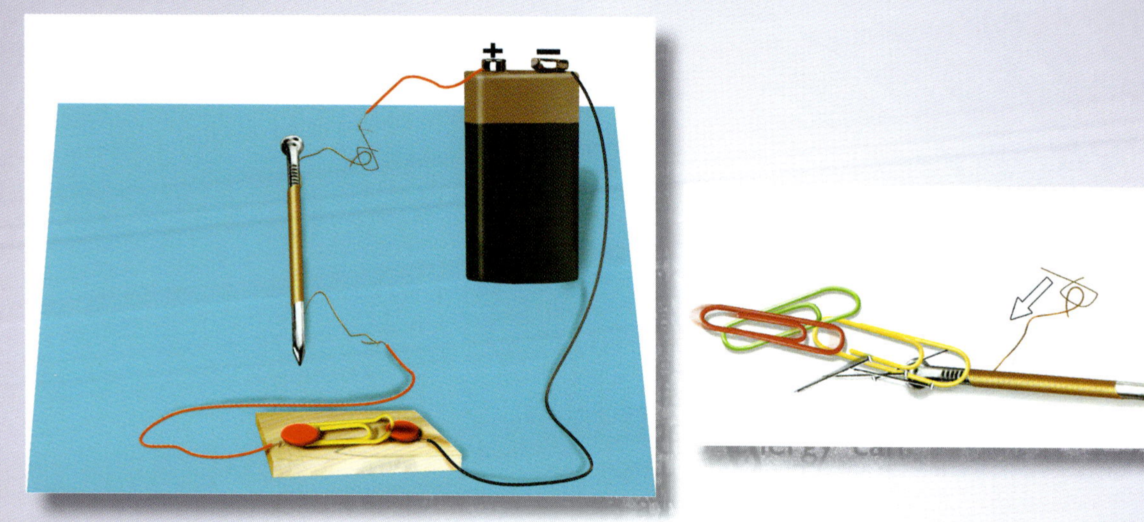

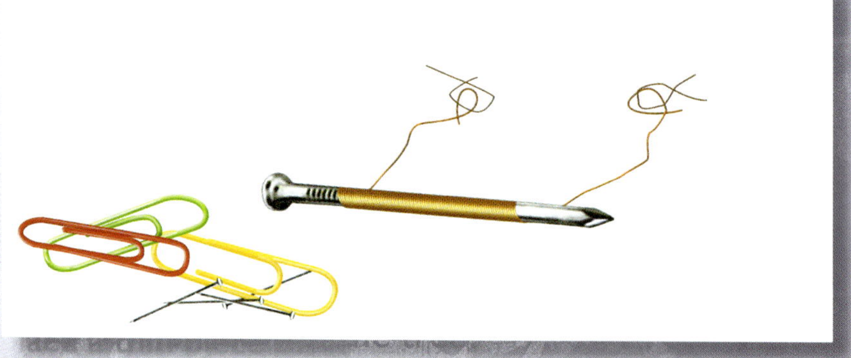

Try this

You may be able to make a piece of soft iron by heating an iron nail to red and letting it cool slowly. Do it with the help of an adult.

Where are electromagnets used?

Electromagnets are found in many things of daily use, such as electric bells, loudspeakers, fans, motors and generators.

In tape recorders a magnet is used to record sound on to the tape. Sound is first converted into an electric current which is passed through the recording head. The recording head is a sensitive electromagnet. The tape is made of a magnetic material. When it is passed through the magnetic field of the head, it gets magnetised and records the variation in the current. This information remains stored in the tape for later use.

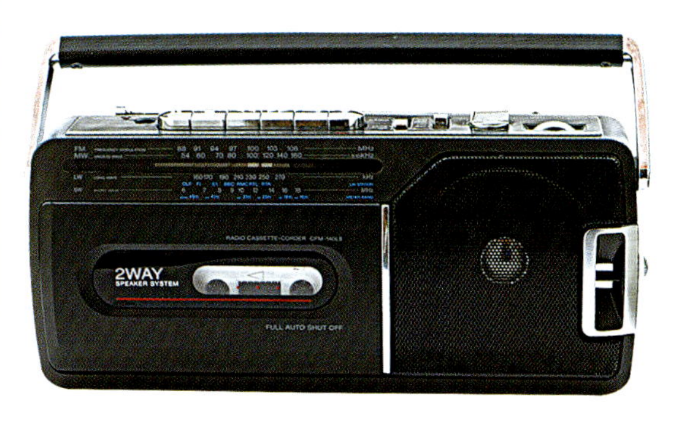

A large electromagnet can be used in a crane for shifting scrap iron. To release the load, the driver has to simply switch off the current to the coils of the electromagnet.

Make a model railway signal

You will need:

- an empty barrel of a ball point pen
- a nail
- insulated wire
- a 9-volt battery
- sellotape
- an ON-OFF switch
- a cardboard box
- a 6-inch wooden scale
- coloured paper
- thread

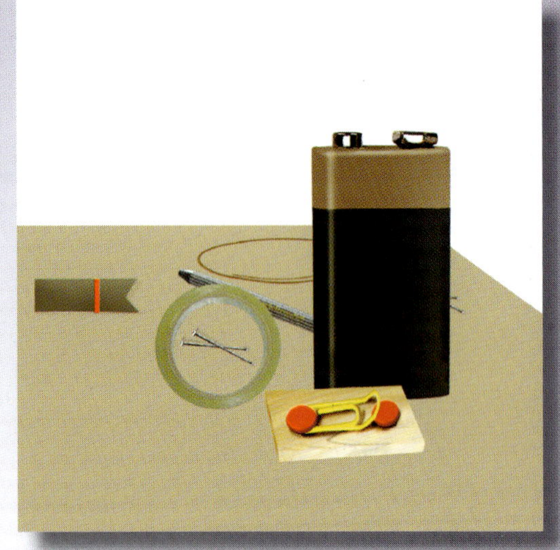

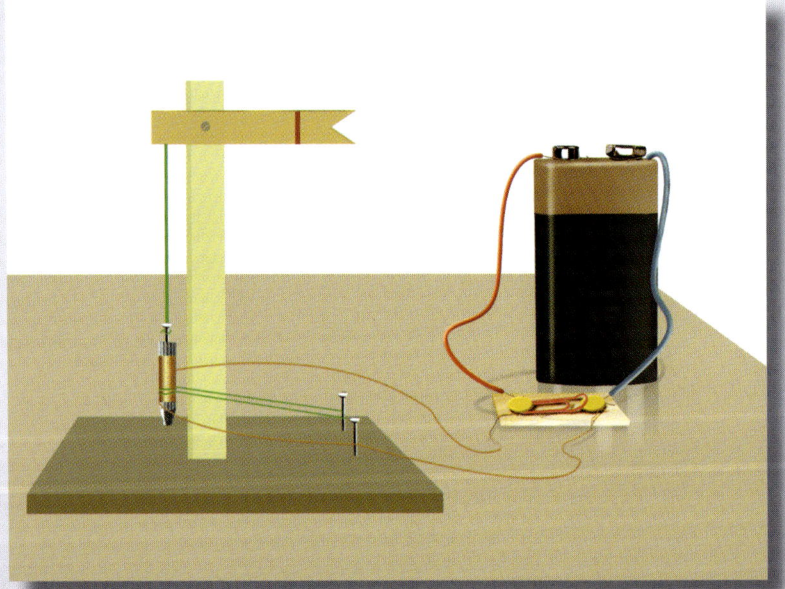

1. Fix the barrel of the pen to the cardboard box.
2. Fix the scale to the cardboard box as shown. Make a flag and pin it to the scale so that it can move easily.
3. Tie a thread to the flag and attach a nail to the other end of the thread. The nail should go in and out of the barrel as the flag goes up and down.
4. Wrap 100 turns of wire around the tube and connect one end to the battery as shown. Connect the other end of this battery through the switch.
5. Press the switch ON and see what happens. The barrel electromagnet will draw the nail towards it and thus raise the flag. (Do not keep the switch on for more than a few seconds. It will drain your battery.)